Past and Present

Astronomy Today

BY ISAAC ASIMOV
WITH REVISIONS AND UPDATING BY RICHARD HANTULA

Gareth Stevens Publishing
A WORLD ALMANAC EDUCATION GROUP COMPANY

Please visit our web site at: www.garethstevens.com
For a free color catalog describing Gareth Stevens Publishing's list of high-quality books and multimedia programs, call 1-800-542-2595 (USA) or 1-800-387-3178 (Canada). Gareth Stevens Publishing's fax: (414) 332-3567.

Library of Congress Cataloging-in-Publication Data

Asimov, Isaac.
Astronomy today / by Isaac Asimov; with revisions and updating by Richard Hantula.
p. cm. — (Isaac Asimov's 21st century library of the universe. Past and present)
Includes bibliographical references and index.
ISBN 0-8368-3980-3 (lib. bdg.)
1. Astronomy—Juvenile literature. I. Hantula, Richard. II. Title.
QB46.A78 2005
520—dc22 2005049030

This edition first published in 2006 by
Gareth Stevens Publishing
A Member of the WRC Media Family of Companies
330 West Olive Street, Suite 100
Milwaukee, WI 53212 USA

Series editor: Mark J. Sachner
Art direction: Tammy West
Cover design: Melissa Valuch
Layout adaptation: Melissa Valuch and Jenni Gaylord
Picture research: Matthew Groshek
Additional picture research: Diane Laska-Swanke
Production director: Jessica Morris
Production coordinator: Robert Kraus

The editors at Gareth Stevens Publishing have selected science author Richard Hantula to bring this classic series of young people's information books up to date. Richard Hantula has written and edited books and articles on science and technology for more than two decades. He was the senior U.S. editor for the *Macmillan Encyclopedia of Science.*

In addition to Hantula's contribution to this most recent edition, the editors would like to acknowledge the participation of two noted science authors, Greg Walz-Chojnacki and Francis Reddy, as contributors to earlier editions of this work.

Printed in the United States of America

1 2 3 4 5 6 7 8 9 09 08 07 06 05

Contents

We live in an enormously large place – the Universe. It's only natural that we would want to understand this place, so scientists and engineers have developed instruments and spacecraft that have told us far more about the Universe than we could possibly imagine.

We have seen planets up close, and spacecraft have even landed on some. We have learned about quasars and pulsars, supernovas and colliding galaxies, and black holes and dark matter. We have gathered amazing data about how the Universe may have come into being and how it may end. Nothing could be more astonishing.

Astronomy today makes use of large and complex instruments of many kinds. But it is practiced in simpler ways, as well. Astronomy is a science in which all people – young and not-so-young, amateur and professional – can participate. Even with basic instruments, such as binoculars and telescopes, the Universe is open to everyone!

Gazing Skyward

In ancient times, astronomers simply gazed skyward to make their discoveries. Without any special tools, they learned a great deal about the Sun, Moon, and planets (that is, those planets that could be seen with the naked eye). They also determined the length of a year and developed calendars.

Today, astronomers still observe the sky. But they have new ways of gathering information and new ideas about how the Universe works. For example, modern astronomers use instruments that can collect vast amounts of light and also instruments that study the kinds of radiation that are invisible to the eye. Astronomers today also use modern technology to determine such things as how stars came to be, how they change with time, and how they will come to an end.

Below: Stonehenge, near Salisbury in England, is one of a number of stone structures built by ancient people over the past several thousands years ago that, some scientists think, may have been used to help track the movements of celestial bodies.

A misty path called the Milky Way cuts through the darkness of the night sky. The Milky Way is the combined light of billions of stars. *Inset:* The human eye detects only visible light, but scientific instruments reveal the presence of other types of radiation beyond the red and violet ends of the visible spectrum.

Above: A South Korean postage stamp celebrates an ancient observatory.

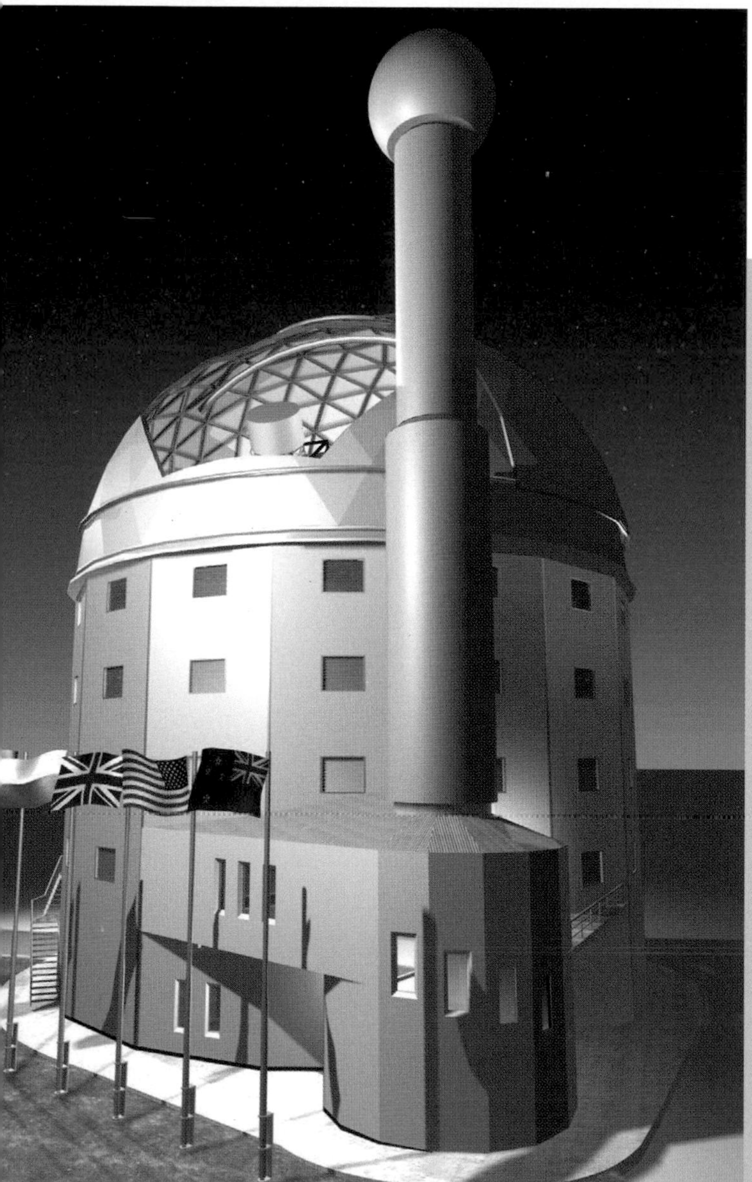

Top: The twin Keck I and Keck II telescopes on the Hawaiian mountain Mauna Kea can be linked by computer to act like a single huge telescope.

Above: A view of the dim binary, or double, star system called HK Tau made by the Keck II telescope in 2003 using infrared light. The image not only reveals the two separate parts of the system but also shows hints of a disk of dust and gas surrounding the smaller star.

Left: An artist's drawing of the Southern African Large Telescope (SALT), located near Sutherland, South Africa. The telescope, sponsored by several countries, was scheduled to be completed in 2005. The main mirror — actually a combination of 91 smaller mirrors — is 36 feet (11 m) wide, making SALT the biggest single telescope in the Southern Hemisphere.

New Eyes on the Sky

For a long time, the great telescope on Palomar Mountain in California, which went into operation in 1949, was the largest telescope on Earth. It uses a mirror that is 200 inches (5 meters) across. In recent years, however, scientists have been using new methods to build much larger telescopes.

On the Hawaiian mountain of Mauna Kea, there are two 400-inch (10-m) telescopes, called Keck I and Keck II. They can be linked by computer to act as a single telescope much bigger than the Palomar "giant!" The main mirror in each of the Kecks is a combination of 36 smaller mirrors. This sounds complicated, but it is much easier to do than making one huge mirror.

Another multi-telescope giant is the Very Large Telescope in Chile. It consists of four 320-inch (8.2-m) telescopes that can be used separately or operated together as a single super instrument.

Above: The 200-inch (5-m) telescope on Palomar Mountain in California.

Earth's atmosphere is a problem for astronomers. It distorts their view of the sky. One way around this problem is to use flying observatories – specially equipped planes that carry telescopes for observing the Universe from high in the atmosphere. This is especially valuable for observation using infrared radiation, most of which is absorbed by water vapor in the atmosphere before it reaches the ground. NASA planned to start regular operation of the world's biggest airborne telescope in 2006: a 98.4-inch (2.5-m) infrared telescope developed by German scientists.

A Clear Picture

It doesn't matter whether the telescope you use is in an observatory or in your bedroom window – there will be times when visibility will be poor. Clouds and fog can hide the sky. The atmosphere can absorb and scatter light so you cannot see the stars. Even on clear nights, the air can be unsteady, causing the stars to "quiver."

That is why astronomers build observatories on mountaintops or other high locations, where the seeing is much better. Big modern telescopes also tend to have special equipment that can help compensate for atmospheric distortion. Other ways of getting around the problem are to put telescopes in space, where there is no atmosphere, or on airplanes that fly high in the sky, where atmospheric distortion is less. But space telescopes are very expensive, and planes cannot carry very large telescopes and are able to stay aloft for only a limited time.

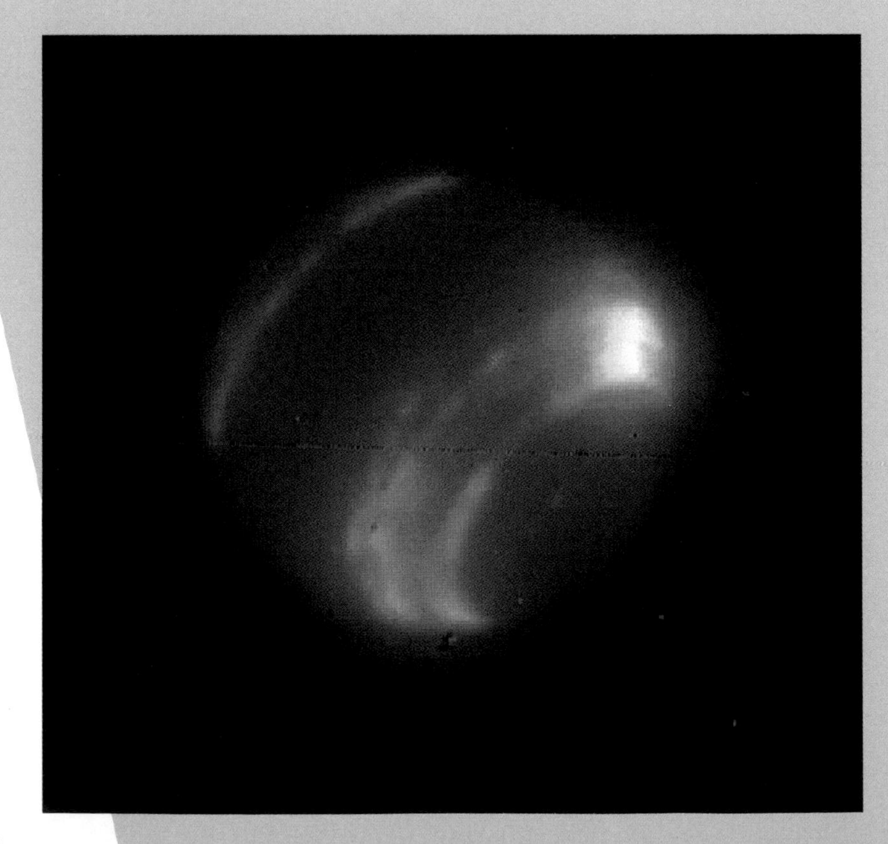

Left: Special "adaptive optics" technology can reduce the distortions caused by the atmosphere in telescope images. This picture of the planet Neptune was made with the Keck II telescope in Hawaii using adaptive optics.

Above: One type of adaptive optics uses a laser beam to help detect atmospheric distortions in order to make adjustments for them. The laser beam shown here, rising from the Keck II telescope in Hawaii, is ordinarily not visible to the eye. In order to photograph it, a very long exposure was used.

Observatories are often built on mountaintops, where telescopes can look through the clean, dry air above the clouds.

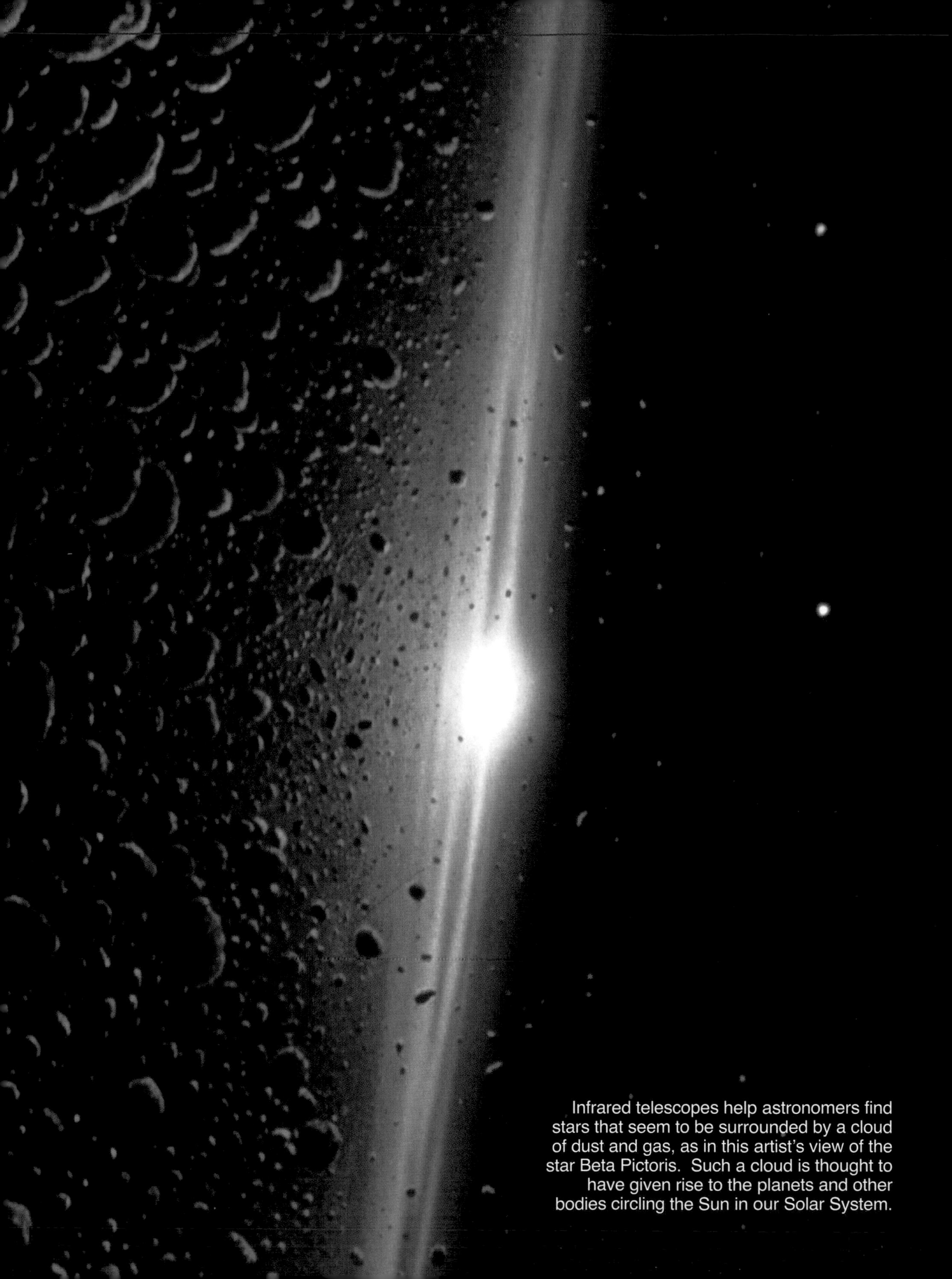

Infrared telescopes help astronomers find stars that seem to be surrounded by a cloud of dust and gas, as in this artist's view of the star Beta Pictoris. Such a cloud is thought to have given rise to the planets and other bodies circling the Sun in our Solar System.

Listening to the Radio . . . Waves!

Besides light, the types of radiation given off by stars and galaxies include radio waves. Astronomers use special radio telescopes to receive and concentrate radio waves.

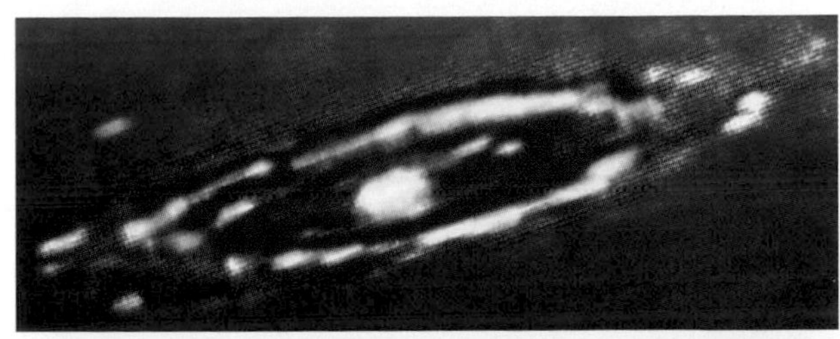

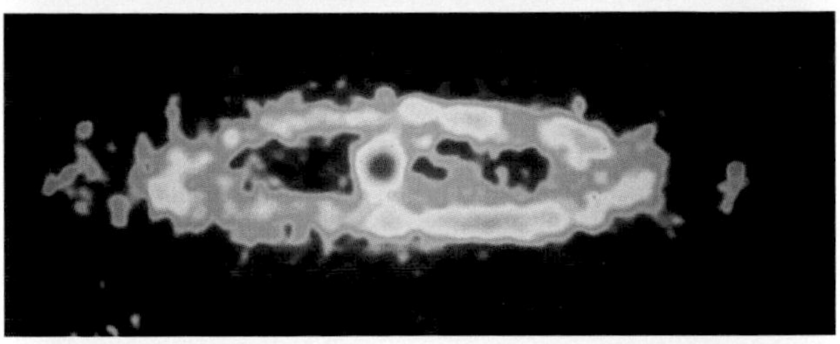

Above: M31, the closest spiral galaxy to Earth — as seen by infrared waves *(top)*, radio waves *(center)*, and visible light *(bottom)*.

Radio waves transmit certain information that light does not. For example, radio waves have helped astronomers detect very distant objects called quasars and tiny, rapidly rotating stars called pulsars. Black holes in the center of galaxies and various chemicals in clouds of dust between stars have been discovered with the assistance of radio waves.

Infrared waves are another type of radiation observed by astronomers. They carry heat energy and have played an important role in the search for planets around distant stars.

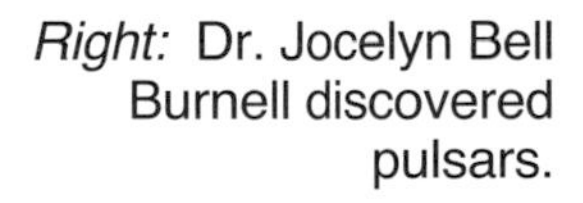

Right: Dr. Jocelyn Bell Burnell discovered pulsars.

Would you believe . . . Little Green Men!

In 1967, a young British astronomer, Jocelyn Bell Burnell, helped develop a huge radio telescope made of 2,048 antennae. She noticed that some of the radio signals picked up by this telescope were extremely steady — so steady that scientists wondered if the signals came from an intelligent source. The signals were given the nickname LGM, for "Little Green Men." But they were too steady to be of intelligent origin. Bell Burnell had discovered pulsars — rapidly spinning neutron stars that send out radiation such as radio waves with each turn.

An array of small radio telescopes can be joined by computer to function as one giant "superscope."

An astronomer studies an image produced by a combination of radio telescopes.

The Superscope Age

Scientists use computers to join a number of small telescopes into one large telescope. In this way, radio telescopes that may be up to thousands of miles apart combine and become more powerful than any single radio telescope.

Computers can also analyze the light that telescopes receive and study it with greater precision than the human eye or cameras can. Thanks to computers, astronomers can now see dim stars, remote galaxies, and other distant objects in the sky more sharply than ever before.

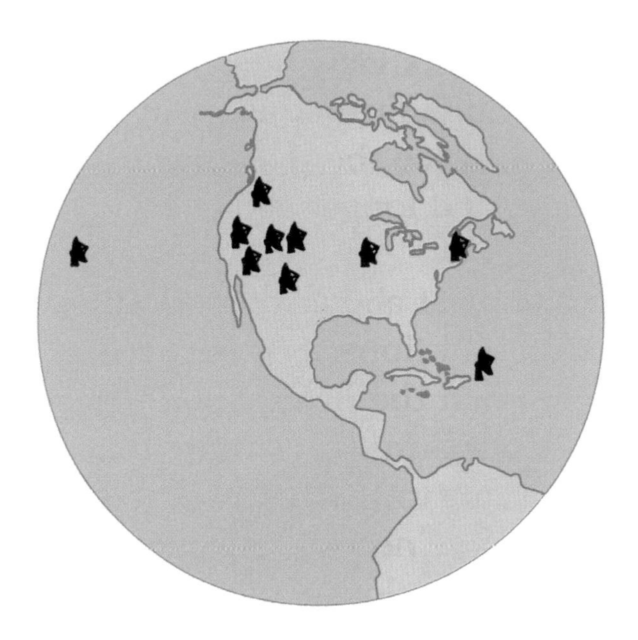

Above: A map showing the huge network of radio telescopes called the Very Long Baseline Array. The network stretches more than 5,000 miles (8,000 km). Its ten radio telescopes — each about 82 feet (25 m) wide — can work together as a single massive instrument.

Above: A collection of radio telescopes near Socorro, New Mexico, called the Very Large Array. The telescopes are movable, and each arm of the VLA can be up to 13 miles (21 km) long.

Space Telescopes

The atmosphere can cause difficulties for astronomers on Earth who want to observe light from stars, galaxies, and so forth. But the difficulties are not limited to light. The atmosphere hampers or even blocks some other types of radiation from reaching Earth's surface. An ideal way to avoid these problems is to make observations from space – beyond the atmosphere.

Remote-controlled instruments for observing the Universe have been placed in various orbits by NASA, the European Space Agency, and other space agencies. They include telescopes that can produce images using light or other types of electromagnetic radiation, such as infrared waves, ultraviolet rays, X rays, and gamma rays.

NASA launched a series of four such spacecraft called the Great Observatories. They are the Hubble Space Telescope (launched in 1990); the Compton Gamma Ray Observatory (in orbit from 1991 to 2000); the Chandra X-Ray Observatory (launched in 1999); and the Spitzer Space Telescope (launched in 2003), for infrared observations.

Above: The Hubble Space Telescope in orbit above Earth.

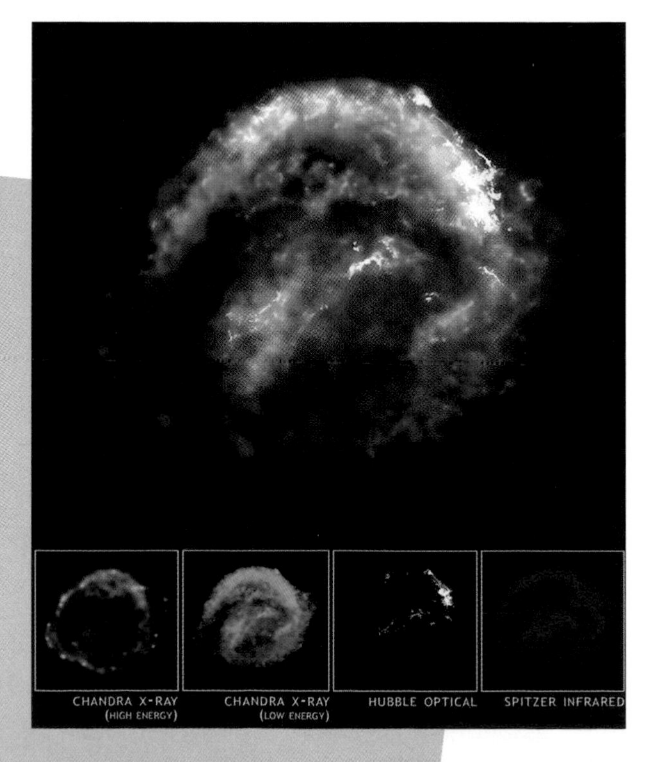

Right: Masses of gas and dust surround the remains of a star whose explosion in a supernova was observed in 1604. This vivid picture was made by combining X-ray, infrared, and optical observations from the Chandra, Spitzer, and Hubble space observatories.

Top: The Spitzer Space Telescope (for infrared observations) orbits the Sun. It is depicted here in front of an infrared view of our Milky Way Galaxy.

Left: The Chandra X-Ray Observatory orbiting high above Earth.

Bottom: Some of the galaxies visible in this image from the Hubble Space Telescope are too faint to be seen from Earth's surface. The most distant ones are up to 13 billion light-years from Earth.

A Worthwhile Watch

Being a professional astronomer may sound like fun, but it is also very hard work. It may mean spending countless hours studying data for days, weeks, and even months on end.

Astronomers are not the only people who take part in the job of keeping watch on the skies. Technicians run the computer systems, operate the telescopes, handle the cameras, develop the films, analyze the light, and carry out other related tasks.

What's more, big telescopes are located in out-of-the-way, often remote places. Most are built on mountains or other high areas in order to "see" above the thickest, dirtiest part of Earth's atmosphere. An observatory can be a cold place in which to work, because heating it can make the air quiver and distort the image in a scope

But the excitement of making a new, important discovery in the skies makes everyone's hard work worthwhile.

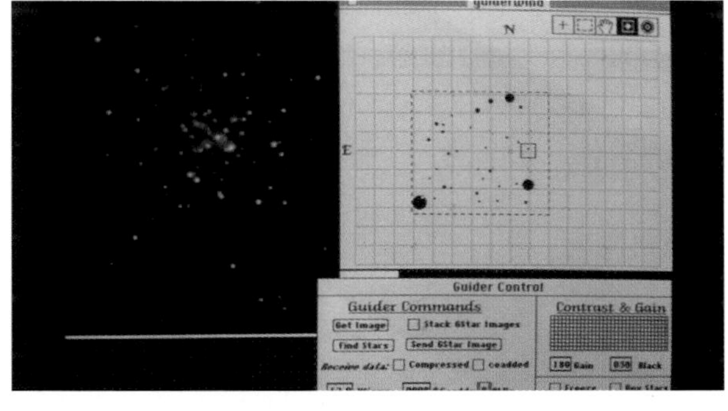

Above: An astronomer photographs the Sun in the 1920s.

Right top: In modern times, a computer screen displays the view through a large telescope.

Right bottom: This 138-inch (3.5-m) telescope at Apache Point Observatory in New Mexico went into operation in 1994. It was the first large telescope on Earth that could be operated completely by remote control — in other words, astronomers did not need to actually be at the observatory.

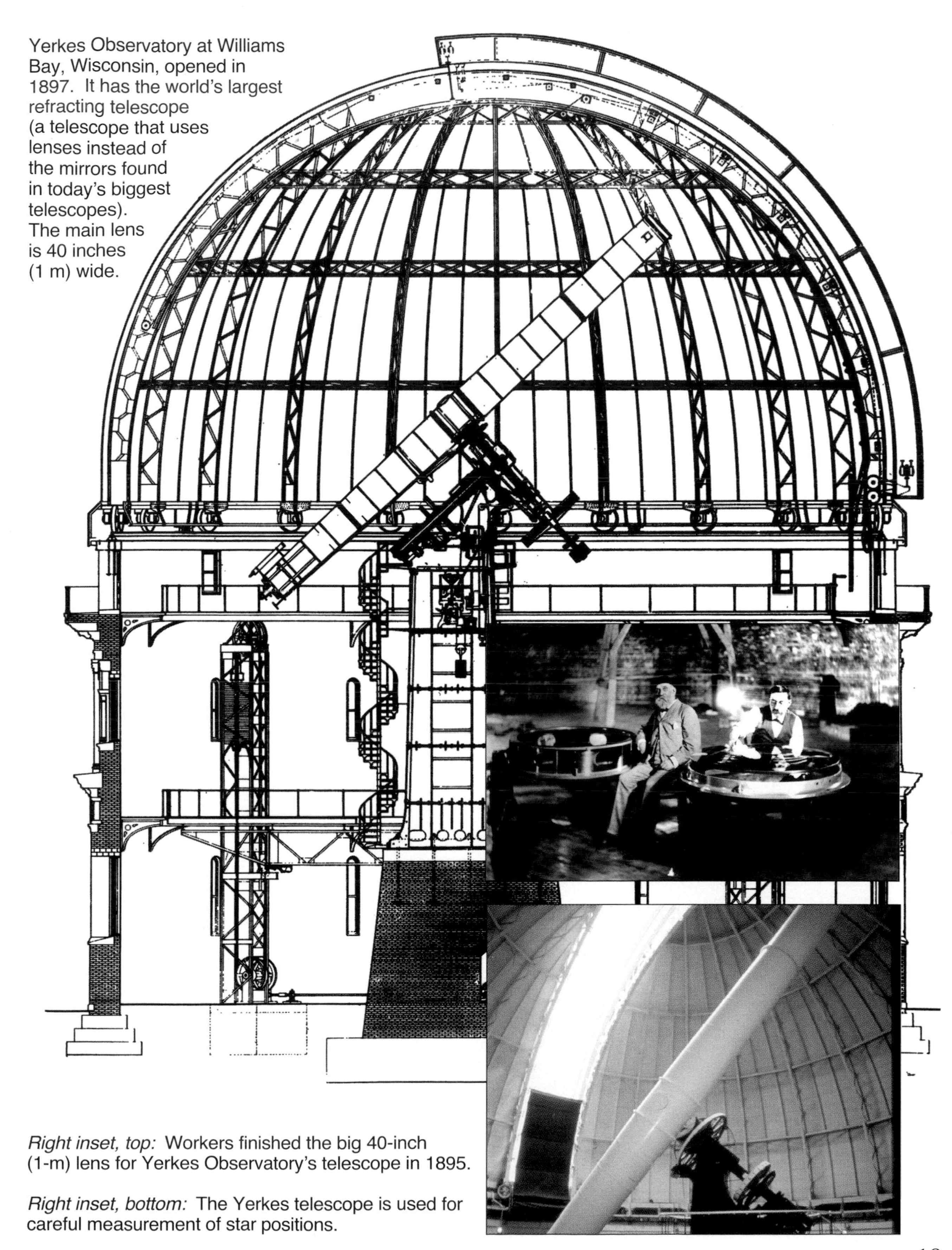

Yerkes Observatory at Williams Bay, Wisconsin, opened in 1897. It has the world's largest refracting telescope (a telescope that uses lenses instead of the mirrors found in today's biggest telescopes). The main lens is 40 inches (1 m) wide.

Right inset, top: Workers finished the big 40-inch (1-m) lens for Yerkes Observatory's telescope in 1895.

Right inset, bottom: The Yerkes telescope is used for careful measurement of star positions.

An artist imagines Phobos, one of the moons of Mars.

Astronomer E. E. Barnard at Yerkes Observatory.

Amateurs and Their Professional Work

Important discoveries have been made by astronomers who were amateurs or who began their career as amateurs.

Asaph Hall was a carpenter who loved astronomy. He became an assistant at the Harvard College Observatory in Massachusetts and later got a job at the U.S. Naval Observatory in Washington, D.C., where he discovered the moons of Mars in 1877.

Clyde Tombaugh was too poor to go to college, but he managed to get a job as an assistant at Lowell Observatory in Arizona, where he discovered the planet Pluto in 1930.

Jay McNeil, a satellite TV dish installer in Kentucky, in 2004 discovered a new nebula (a cloud of gas and dust) where a star was being born. The cloud is now called McNeil's Nebula.

Right: Asaph Hall, who discovered the moons of Mars.

Far right: McNeil's Nebula, a cloud of gas and dust discovered by amateur astronomer Jay McNeil with a small telescope in 2004.

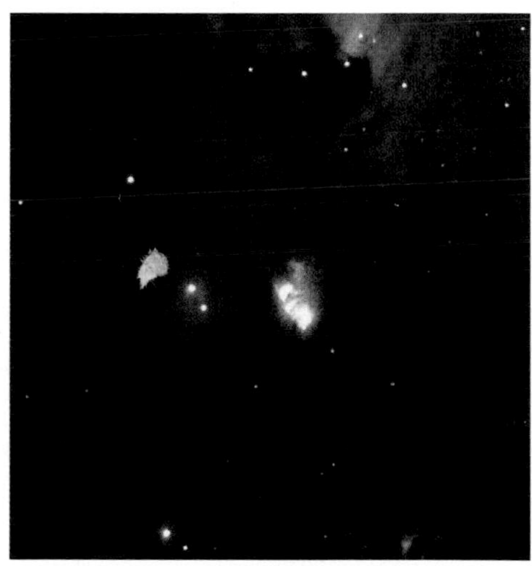

The most eagle-eyed amateur astronomer of all may have been E. E. Barnard. He was such an enthusiastic observer that he was given a job as a professional astronomer. In 1892 he became the first person to discover a moon of Jupiter in almost three centuries. He could barely detect it because it was so near the planet's bright light. Barnard also thought he saw craters on Mars. He didn't officially announce his find, because he thought he would be laughed at. Much later, in 1965, pictures taken by a space probe showed Mars really does have craters.

Sciences Combine in the Cosmos

Astronomy takes equipment, patience, and luck. But it also takes a lot of thinking about science and mathematics.

Albert Einstein was not an astronomer, but he developed a theory about how gravity and other forces in the Universe might work. It is called the general theory of relativity. The theory has aided astronomers in their observations of the cosmos. For instance, it has helped them understand unusual motions of planets and odd things that happen to light. One such thing is "gravitational lensing" – light rays that pass near a huge object in space are curved by the object's powerful gravity, as if by a lens.

Today, scientists have theories about how the Universe came into existence. Astronomers are trying to make observations that either prove or disprove these theories.

Left: A sculpture of Albert Einstein in Washington, D.C. Einstein was a physicist who explained how gravity and other forces in the Universe work.

Gravitational lenses – throwing astronomers a curve!

In 1936, Albert Einstein said that if a massive object lay in front of a distant star, then light from that star would curve around the object on its way toward Earth. The gravity of the object would act like a lens As a result, the distant star would appear not as a point, but as a ring. Such a ring is called an "Einstein ring." In 1987, about half a century after Einstein explained how a gravitational lens could bend light into a ring, the first Einstein ring was discovered with the help of radio telescope data. The ring that was observed turned out to be a remote quasar, and the object acting as a lens in front of it was a galaxy.

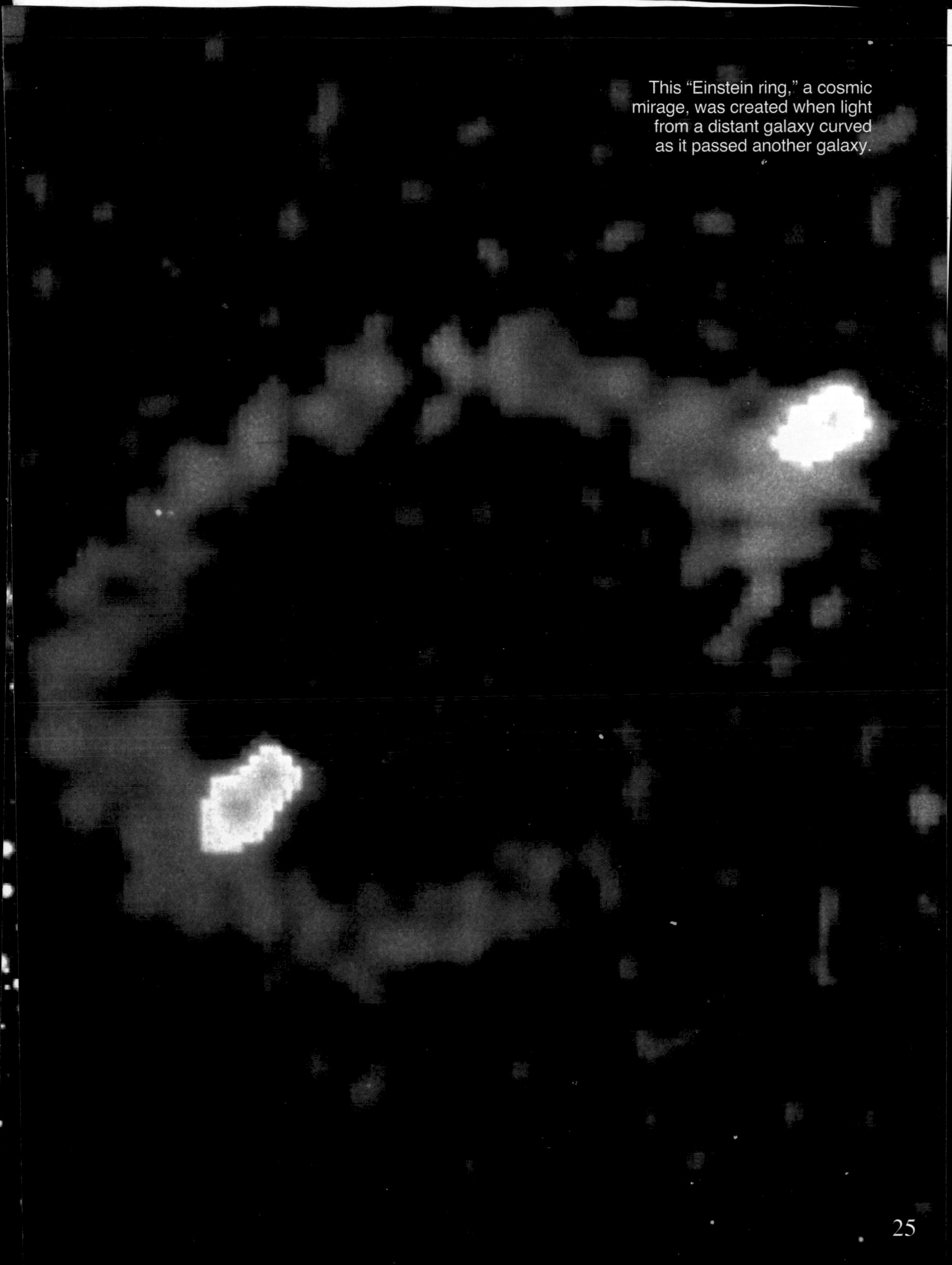

This "Einstein ring," a cosmic mirage, was created when light from a distant galaxy curved as it passed another galaxy.

Fact File: The Spectrum

The Sun, planets, and stars are sources of visible light that looks rather white. But there is another form of visible light – the spectrum. This is light that is refracted, or broken up, into the band of colors that together make up white light. The colors of the visible spectrum can be seen through a prism and in a rainbow.

When white light is broken up into its colors, information is revealed about the source of the light. For example, by examining the light of a distant galaxy with a special tool called a spectroscope, astronomers can determine whether that galaxy is moving away from Earth or toward Earth – and how fast. Light waves from a celestial body coming toward Earth are shorter, and move, or shift, toward what is called the violet end of the spectrum. Light waves from a celestial body moving away from Earth are longer, and shift toward the red end of the spectrum.

Light waves are one type of electromagnetic radiation. Scientists also study types of electromagnetic radiation that are invisible to the human eye. These types exist beyond the colors of

White light refracted through a prism.

The Invisible Spectrum – Violet End:

Johann Wilhelm Ritter (1776-1810), a German scientist, discovered ultraviolet radiation in tests performed on chemicals that later became widely used to make photographs.

Cyril Hazard, a British radio astronomer, located a strong source of ultraviolet radiation with a huge redshift in 1962. This redshift indicated that the object — a quasar — was moving away from Earth at great speed and was at a great distance from our planet.

Explorer 42 (also called *Uhuru*), a U.S. satellite launched from Kenya in 1970 to observe X rays, found some of the first real evidence for the existence of black holes.

The Visible Spectrum:

Sir Isaac Newton (1642-1727), an English scientist, refracted white light through a prism into red, orange, yellow, green, blue, and violet — the spectrum. He was the first to explain light as a pattern of bright lines of different colors.

Joseph von Fraunhofer (1787-1826), a German optician, developed a way of showing the spectrum more clearly, as a series of distinct vertical lines of color, as well as dark lines, called spectral lines. He combined the prism and the telescope into the spectroscope and with it discovered that the spectral lines of the Moon and planets are the same as those of the Sun. This proved that light from the Moon and planets is, in fact, reflected sunlight.

the spectrum. For example, beyond the violet end of the spectrum lie ultraviolet radiation, X rays, and gamma rays. And beyond the red end of the spectrum lie infrared radiation, microwaves, and radio waves.

All forms of electromagnetic radiation, including visible color, involve waves. These waves can be measured according to their different wavelengths. In astronomy, they are detected with telescopes or with radio telescopes and other special instruments, depending on their wavelength. By studying the information gathered by instruments, astronomers learn about objects in the Universe, such as black holes, that cannot be visited, or even seen, from Earth.

Although rockets can be sent to other worlds to collect information, astronomy is still an observational science. This means it is dependent on the gathering of light and other radiation from distant sources. Because of the visible and invisible spectrum, scientists can learn about the farthest reaches of the Universe without having to actually visit those places.

Armand H. L. Fizeau (1819-1896), a French scientist, used a spectroscope in 1848 to show whether an object is moving toward Earth (violet shift) or away from Earth (red shift) — and how fast.

Robert Wilhelm Bunsen (1811-1899) and Gustav Robert Kirchoff (1824-1887), German scientists, used a burner developed by and named after Bunsen to determine that certain elements give off bright or dark lines. This meant that light from a star could be analyzed to determine more than just brightness, position, and motion — but chemical makeup, as well.

Wilhelm Wien (1864-1928), a German scientist, found a relation between spectral color and temperature that astronomers could use to measure star temperatures.

Annie Jump Cannon (1863-1941), an American astronomer, used spectrographic methods to classify stars in order of decreasing temperature.

Vesto Melvin Slipher (1875-1969), an American astronomer, discovered that most galaxies show a redshift, meaning they are moving away from Earth. This discovery contributed to the "Big Bang" theory of the birth of the Universe.

The Invisible Spectrum – Red End:

William Herschel (1738-1822), a German-born English astronomer, discovered infrared radiation by detecting heat beyond the red end of the spectrum. This meant there must be a type of radiation beyond red — infrared — that cannot be seen.

Heinrich Rudolf Hertz (1857-1894), a German scientist, detected wavelengths much longer than infrared radiation — radio waves.

Karl Guthe Jansky (1905-1950), an American radio engineer, detected a radio "hiss" coming from the center of our Galaxy. His discovery led to the birth of radio astronomy.

Jocelyn Bell Burnell, a British astronomer, detected rapid pulses of radio waves from a star in 1967. She discovered rapidly spinning, densely packed neutron stars, or pulsars.

More Books about Astronomy Today

A to Z of Scientists in Space and Astronomy. Deborah Todd and Joseph A. Angelo Jr. (Facts on File)

The Firefly Encyclopedia Of Astronomy. Paul Murdin and Margaret Penston (Firefly)

Hubble: The Mirror on the Universe. Robin Kerrod (Firefly)

Observing the Universe. Ray Spangenburg, Kit Moser (Franklin Watts)

A Stargazer's Guide. Isaac Asimov (Gareth Stevens)

The Universe: 365 Days. Robert J. Nemiroff, Jerry T. Bonnell (Abrams)

DVDs

Stargaze – Hubble's View of the Universe. (DVD International)

Stargaze II – Visions of the Universe. (Wea)

Starry Night: Searching for SuperStars. (Imaginova)

Web Sites

The Internet is a good place to get more information about Astronomy. The web sites listed here can help you learn about the most recent discoveries, as well as those made in the past.

Chandra X-Ray Observatory Center. chandra.harvard.edu/

HubbleSite. hubblesite.org/

NASA, Imagine the Universe. imagine.gsfc.nasa.gov/

National Radio Astronomy Observatory. www.nrao.edu/epo/

Spitzer Space Telescope. www.spitzer.caltech.edu/

Windows to the Universe. http://www.windows.ucar.edu/

Places to Visit

You can explore the Universe without leaving Earth. Here are some museums and centers where you can find exhibits on a variety of aspects of astronomy.

Adler Planetarium and Astronomy Museum
1300 S. Lake Shore Drive
Chicago, Illinois 60605-2403

American Museum of Natural History
Rose Center for Earth and Space
Central Park West at 79th Street
New York, NY 10024

Morehead Planetarium and Science Center
259 East Franklin Street
Chapel Hill, North Carolina 27599

Museum of Science, Boston
Science Park
Boston, Massachusetts 02114

National Air and Space Museum
Smithsonian Institution
6th and Independence Avenue SW
Washington, DC 20560

Scienceworks Museum
2 Booker Street, Spotswood
Melbourne, Victoria 3015
Australia

Glossary

amateur: a person who engages in an art, science, or sport for enjoyment rather than profit.

astronomer: a person involved in the scientific study of the Universe and its various celestial bodies.

atmosphere: the gases that surround a planet, star, or moon.

billion: the number represented by 1 followed by nine zeroes — 1,000,000,000.

black hole: a tightly packed object with such powerful gravity that not even light can escape from it.

calendar: a system for dividing time, most commonly into days, weeks, and months.

comet: a small object in space made of ice, rock, and dust. When its orbit brings it closer to the Sun, it develops a tail of gas and dust.

crater: a hole or pit on a planet or moon created by the impact of an object or by a volcanic explosion.

electromagnetic radiation: such forms of radiation as gamma rays, X rays, ultraviolet radiation, light, infrared radiation, radio waves, and microwaves.

galaxy: a large star system containing up to hundreds of billions of stars. Our own galaxy is known as the Milky Way.

gravity: the force that causes objects like Earth and the Moon to be drawn to one another.

light-year: the distance that light travels in one year — nearly 6 trillion miles (9.5 trillion km).

NASA: the National Aeronautics and Space Administration — the government space agency in the United States.

nebula: a cloud of gas and dust in space.

neutron star: a star that has as much mass as an ordinary large star, but the mass — consisting mainly of the nuclear particles called neutrons — is squeezed into a much smaller ball.

nova: a star that suddenly increases greatly in brightness, as much as a thousand times or more, and then becomes dimmer again over a few weeks, months, or years.

orbit: the path that one celestial object follows as it circles, or revolves around, another.

pulsar: a neutron star that sends out rapid pulses of light or other radiation.

quasar: an extremely distant object that seems to resemble a star and gives off huge amounts of energy. Quasars seem to be located at the centers of galaxies and involve an enormous black hole.

radio telescope: an instrument that uses a radio receiver and antenna to see into space and listen for signals from space.

radio waves: electromagnetic waves that can be detected by radio-receiving equipment.

redshift: the apparent reddening of the light given off by an object moving away from us. The greater the redshift of light from a distant galaxy, the farther away the galaxy is located and the faster it is moving away from us.

satellite: an object in space that orbits a larger object.

supernova: the explosion of a star during which the star may become a million or more times brighter.

telescope: an instrument with lenses or mirrors for viewing distant objects.